WHAT I LEARNED IN PRISON...

Out of the darkness into the light.

Tracy McFadden

What I learned in Prison…

Out of the darkness into the light.

Dedication

First and foremost, to my Lord and Savior Jesus Christ who continues to relentlessly pursue me.

My mom without whom I would not be here. She gave me the beautiful traits of tenacity and strength.

My husband who is an extraordinary example of unconditional love to me every single day.

Kathy the first friend God put in my life who accepted me as I was and loved me enough to not let me stay there.

My Connect group family whom through their faithfulness to act on Gods prompting made this book even possible.

Liz Fuerte for being the "midwife" who was instrumental in seeing this book birthed.

Contents

Introduction

The testimonies you are about to read come from a heart that was lost within the darkness that this life can bring, but found light, life, and hope in a knight in shining armor named Jesus. His relentless love afforded me the keys to open the prison doors I found myself behind.

I am a daughter, sister, wife, mother and Memaw. There are no worldly credentials to follow my name. I was lost but now I am found. I was blind but now I see. God changed this ordinary girl from the inside out and I cannot help but share the living water I have found. It quenches thirst and brings me to life, and I know you can find the same peace and comfort in Him.

I pray the words in this book will release the key you need to walk out of whatever prison you may find yourself in. If He can do it for a wretch like me, He can do it for you, too.

I am the Lord; I have called you in righteousness;

I will take you by the hand and keep you;

I will give you as a covenant for the people,

a light for the nations,

to open the eyes that are blind,

to bring out the prisoners from the dungeon,

from the prison those who sit in darkness.

—Isaiah 42: 6-7 (ESV)

Prelude

I do not think you can read this book without first knowing the background to its existence. There was a miracle performed, to confirm that the writing of this book was indeed the very will of God! It is also a beautiful picture of the God you will experience throughout the pages of this book. A God who pursues you and communicates with you in real, tangible and personal ways in order to ensure your purpose is fulfilled. Let me tell you how God showed up and showed off!

God had placed the title of this book on my heart about a year prior what you are holding in your hands today. His perfect timing began to align, and right amid the Covid-19 pandemic, He began to draw me into writing this book. I was led to a free webinar called Project "I AM" Broken to Breakthrough. This led to me applying to Liz Fuerte's program for writing a book in sixty days.

During the webinar, I felt a check in my spirit that God had led me here; however, my financial situation was not in line with this timing. I felt so strongly that God had led me here, I told Liz's team I would pray about it because God would have to make the way. After a very powerful prayer at the closing of our call; I decided to get real with God and began a dialogue with Him.

I struggle with holding tightly to money and trusting you with that part of my life, God. I am currently not working, in the middle of a pandemic and uncertainty so to let me know this is the path you want me to take. I will need something extraordinary to happen, like someone driving up to my house with an envelope full of cash. Amen.

I then went about my day. Less than two hours later, I receive a text from our Connect Group leader asking if I was home because they needed to drop something off. I was outside watering my plants when they pulled up on their golf cart. I walked over to speak with them, and they gave me a bag of left-over biscuits I had paid for during a ministry we had done.

We talked for about twenty minutes and just as they were getting ready to leave, Patrice pulls an envelope out from under her leg and hands it to me.

"What's this?" I ask hardly able to breath at the thought that this envelope contained what I had prayed for just a few hours prior.

She told me she did not know how much money was in the envelope and did not want to know, but the group felt the desire to bless us with this money! I was undone! I had every emotion running through my mind and I was finding it hard to comprehend what was happening. I took the envelope inside and opened it up to find 80% of the money I needed for the program. Immediately, I heard God tell me, "You are right Tracy, you hold very tightly to your money, so you have to release your grip by providing the other 20%. I cannot give you what I have for you with your fist clinched!"

So, this book you are about to read was birthed from a miracle response to prayer of admitted weakness which allowed God's strength to take over. He met me in my uncertainty and fear and busted open the prison doors so I could walk into the freedom of sharing my testimony.

I pray you find freedom from whatever prison you may be locked in today. That is the greatest desire of my heart. I have journeyed from darkness to light and I feel as if I have the key for your freedom, too, within the words of my testimony!

Chapter 1: Loss of Innocence

"You intended to harm me, but God intended it for good to accomplish what is now being done, the saving of many lives." Genesis 50:20 (NIV)

It was just another morning for me and Ms. Beasley, my favorite doll companion, as we entered the kitchen of our babysitter's home. I crawled up into my seat at the small, round table in the center of the kitchen. The smell of eggs and bacon cooking filled the room as I patiently waited for breakfast to be served.

It was a good morning, everything appeared to be peaceful as I sat up on my knees to better reach my plate. But then, he entered the room. I watched him out of the corner of my eye as he went over and took a piece of bacon off the plate sitting on the counter. His mother smiled and told him to have a seat and she would fix him a plate. He glanced over at me with that stupid smirk full of cocky confidence he wore so well. After finishing breakfast, he got up and took his plate over to the sink.

He turned to look at his mom and said, "I am going to take Tracy with me into town today."

My good mood quickly diminished. Fear and anxiety welled up inside of me. I wanted to scream tell her, "NO! Please don't make me go with him today!" It was as if my lips were stitched shut, though. The thoughts were screaming in my head but could not find a place of escape to be freely spoken into the situation. A million wild thoughts of action began to play out in my mind.

Would a stomachache be a valid reason for her to allow me to stay? Maybe a headache? But then resigned to the fact that this little girl had zero power over this man. His mother would never believe the truly dark side of her son.

So, I took his hand as he reached for mine and reluctantly went out the door. This had become something I had to accept. My mind replayed the last time I had gone into town with him, the confusion and uneasiness I had felt when his hand was placed on my private parts. My heart racing and my mind so confused as I was too young to understand what was actually happening. I knew it was not normal and definitely not something I liked. My innocence was taken and my spirit stifled.

I am not sure why I did not tell my parents what was happening in this home. They were loving and protective parents who would have gone to extreme lengths to deal with the situation. In fact, this guy didn't stand a chance against the wrath of my fiercely devoted family! Maybe he sensed that love and devotion himself and that is why he threatened to burn down my house if I told anyone about what he was doing.

Each day I entered that home and sat in that kitchen another small piece of my identity was stripped away. Fear and silence were the weapons the enemy used to keep me bound in an emotional and spiritual prison. I became very withdrawn and felt completely helpless. What seemed like an eternity was, in reality, only a few short months. I vividly remember standing out on the sidewalk seeing the flames bellowing from the top of the garage, hearing the sirens of the fire engine as it approached, and my mother running up the sidewalk to hug me, relieved to see that I was okay.

It was in that moment, in the middle of the chaos of the burning garage, the fire trucks, the panic voices all around, I found myself in the loving arms of my mom. I knew in this very moment that, ironically, a home on fire was going to be the very thing that set me free! But even though I was physically free, I was mentally locked in a prison of forever seeing myself as less than, used up, damaged beyond repair, and insignificant, without a voice. A piece of me labeled myself a victim that day and held that title with great vigor. So much so that it dictated many aspects of my developmental years, altering and stifling the person I was supposed to be. My once vivacious and lively personality was replaced with a scared and silenced girl. I was living under the shackles of condemnation.

I have encountered so many women and men who experienced sexual abuse in their childhood. I wonder how many of us are walking around in shackles of fear and silence? We get up, put on our smiles, and attempt to appear normal to the world around us, yet on the inside we have a cancer eating away at the very core of who we are. We felt that if anyone knew the secret we were guarding, then we would be even more ostracized than we already perceive ourselves to be.

We desperately want to have it all together, to be normal, to have normal relationships with members of the opposite sex, to know what it must be like to choose to give your body away. Which just leaves us more hopeless and more frustrated knowing the ringing of the bell cannot be undone.

What if I told you that is not where the story must end?

John 10:10 says, *"The thief does not come except to steal, and to kill, and to destroy but I have come that they may have life and that they may have it more abundantly"* (NKJV)

The reason I am sharing my story and being completely transparent about my journey is so the light can shine in the darkness. There are things in this journey we are on that make no sense. They seem unfair and cruel. They make us question God and his love for us. The truth is that God's love for us is the reason we have free will, the freedom to make a choice to follow God and remain in the light. This also means that there is the choice for evil; and seemingly innocent and good people can get caught in the crossfire. Does that mean that God has abandoned us or does not care?

No!

Just like John 10:10 says, the enemy came to kill, steal and destroy. BUT it doesn't stop there. Jesus came so we not only have life but life more abundantly! Jesus died on the cross to cover the sins of the world.

One of the hardest things to grasp is the ground at the foot of the cross is even ground, all are welcome to receive its cleansing power. We all make mistakes. Our humanness wants to categorize sin in different degrees and levels some more forgivable than others, but there are not levels or criteria for the redemptive blood of Jesus Christ! We are all on completely equal footing. We have all sinned and fallen short of the Glory of God.

The first and most difficult step I had to take in finding freedom from the chains I was bound by was to forgive my abuser! I had to understand the power the enemy had over my life by my un-forgiveness which had metastasized into bitterness and anger. It was when I chose to forgive my abuser and truly understand that it was in this forgiveness, I would find true freedom!

Understand that forgiveness does not justify the injustice that was done to you; but it puts the judgment in the hands of the one who has the authority to condemn. That was the pivotal point for me in being able to begin the journey to healing and restoration of all that was stolen from me. It made room for the truth of God's word to penetrate the deepest crevices of my heart and begin to illuminate the darkness, showing me the light. It was like a two-hundred-pound weight had been lifted off my shoulders. I could breath and I could feel things again. I never dreamed I could reach a point in my life where I would forgive someone who had taken so much from me. Precious things that were never intended to be his, but God in his great love and mercy knew that forgiveness was the gate into the garden of healing.

Prior to forgiving my abuser, I wore my anger and bitterness as daily garments. I found myself lashing out at anything or anyone I saw as "abusive". It was like everything I could not say as a child was now something as an adult, I had the authority to do. I could not stand the site of anyone leveling authority over another person. I had become meek myself and cowered back from anyone with a strong personality. Yet, I became obsessed with trying to maintain control of everything I had the power to control. All of this because my identity, and the authority found within, had been stripped away from me at the tender age of five. Forgiveness opened the flood gates allowing the living water to rapidly flow through me and cleanse the broken areas of my very soul.

Forgiveness does not set the abuser free; he was never bound by it in the first place. You are set free! Unforgiveness only holds you back and God says my child you deserve better than that!

Remember we were created in the image of the trinity (Father, Son, Holy Spirit) that is where our true identity lies.

Romans 6:6 says, *"For we know that our old self was crucified with him so that the body ruled by sin might be done away with, that we should no longer be slaves to sin."*

"In Christ we are a new creation the old has passed away. Behold, the new has come!" 2 Corinthians 5:17

Once we remove the shackles of unforgiveness, the prison door is opened, and we can walk into a new beginning. Jesus came to die on the cross to cover the sin of sexual abuse, among many others. His blood covers a multitude of sin, and it also washes us white as snow. The love of God poured out through the blood of his only son Jesus Christ can redeem any sin committed to us or by us. That is the picture and beauty of the gospel. We must see our situation through the nail scarred hands of Jesus. In this journey called life, we are going to accumulate some scars. But we do not need to be ashamed of them; we need to allow them to be used as testimony of a loving God with healing in his hands. Our scars reflect the healing power found within His scars!

Once I began to allow the healing words of God's truth to penetrate the depths of my soul, a true healing began to take place. I began to understand that the enemy used two tools to keep me in the prison of condemnation, fear, and silence. My holding of this secret allowed it to become an integral part of my identity. My vision and perception of my world from this prison was very limited and only validated by the four walls from which I had determined my safety lied.

The light of truth was like a small window, very high up within the confines of my prison. The window was too high for me to reach and impossible to see through. Forgiveness released me from my chains and thrown open the prison door. Now, I am able to see the fear and silence I had believed to be a death sentence was in fact a mere mirage. The truth was that Jesus came to silence fear! Our father gives us a true identity that can never be taken away! He calls us to be adopted into his family. He wants us to accept the free gift of grace and love that was poured out on the cross for you!

There is no condemnation for those who are in Christ! I was a new creation; my freedom renewed my spirit and gave me the ability to begin to love myself again. The best way I can describe it would be like this: I am in a field full of trees and wildflowers, birds flying around singing. The sun is very bright, yet it feels comfortable and cool. I am a young girl who is running through this field of wildflowers with the biggest smile, carefree, happily picking flowers. As I skip along through this field, in the distance I see Him, my Abba, daddy God! He is smiling with such delight; I can actually feel his love when I look in his eyes. I run to Him, and He picks me up and twirls me around. We both laugh and laugh. Then He puts me down, He takes my hand, and we walk together through this field. He begins to whisper the words of truth, hope, and love back into the empty spots from where they had been stolen.

Redemption and healing are possible! It all starts with the unlocking of the prison door. You can retrieve the key as it is found in the box of your heart labeled forgiveness.

Chapter 2: We are all created equal

"Do not be conformed to this world, but be transformed by the renewal of your mind, that by testing you may discern what is the will of God, what is good and acceptable and perfect" Romans 12:2 (ESV)

Just a kindergarten girl walking to her car at the end of the school day, having a little skip in her step as she walked with her new friend, Roger, who was nice enough to carry her books to the car. Excited to introduce her new friend to her parents, not expecting the reactions she received! Too young to understand the timeframe she was growing up in yet having to process the reality that a black boy carrying a white girl's books to the car was not an acceptable behavior. Yet, more difficult was understanding from an innocent and naïve child's point of view what I would tell my new friend when he asked to carry my books again.

In my younger years growing up in the South, I experienced first-hand the segregation of blacks and whites. There were a few restaurants that had a back entrance for people of color. As I grew older the blatant segregation of black and white began to subside, but the effects of navigating through that time span alters your way of thinking to one extreme or the other.

I believe I was born with a very empathetic heart, so my experience in my younger years lead me to have compassion over the situation and drove me to teach my children not to see color, but to see a person for who they are and not what color their skin is. I was determined to break generational chains! Unity, not division, would be the banner I would hold high over my family. The prison of segregation is not one I wanted to raise my family in.

Racism is something that seems to want to hold on with a death grip. This has been passed down in one fashion or another from generation to generation, on and on and on. The problem is not racism, it is sin! Hate, pride, ignorance and the list of sins continue indefinitely. Until the root issue, which is sin, is dealt with and extracted the turmoil between the different ethnicities will forever be a reality. Love and humility are the water hoses that will extinguish the fires of hate and pride; self-righteousness is the gasoline that allows this issue disguised as racism to be a fire fueled into destructive and unproductive behavior.

The key to unlocking the prison door of segregation and hate is the renewal of our minds! Just like Romans 12:2 says we must no longer be conformed to this world, but be transformed by the renewal of your mind... The mindset of the world, possibly even the mindset you were raised to believe, has to be changed. The old way of thinking must be replaced with a renewed way of seeing things. We must allow the truth of God's word to overcome the way we are programmed to think.

Like I mentioned, I raised my kids with the pretense of being "color blind" attempting to protect them from conforming to the way the world. God corrected me on that thought process. He remined me that he created all people in his image and their own unique design. That includes the color of our skin. It has purpose and significance. God created diversity by design but never intended it for division. The very display of his love is unity in our diversity so there is no wonder the enemy would go to great lengths to keep us in the prison of segregation and hate. It is within this prison he can contain the spread of God's love and prolong his eternal destiny in the pit of Hell.

We as children of God must be the light that leads people out of this prison of darkness and expose the lie and the mirage for what it truly is.

Minds need to be transformed with truth for love to be displayed. Love conquers hate.

"Let love be genuine, abhor what is evil; hold fast to what is good." Romans 12:9. God knitted us in our mother's womb with distinct characteristics and features, from the color of our hair to our distinct fingerprints, we are all uniquely designed. It was never the intention of the creator that the creation be defined by their uniqueness but rather their uniqueness define them as beautiful individuals in a diverse and beautifully crafted world. How have we allowed the color of our skin to be the defining adjective to who we are? The true definition of who we are is simply this; we are children of God. The color of our skin is no more defining than the color of our hair; however, us women are always changing that as well, as if Gods natural design is flawed somehow and we must go to great effort and expense to correct Him!

This issue of racism is not just a sin problem it is also an identity problem. Every day when we get up and look in the mirror, we are not defining ourselves as wonderfully complex and exquisitely designed by the creator of the universe! We are allowing our minds to be manipulated to see the glaring flaws that the world wants to falsely accuse us of having. When we believe the lies, we recess into the darkness of not knowing and standing tall in the truth! We cannot allow the enemy to distort the clear view of whose we are! Standing tall in knowing we are perfectly imperfect!

We are designed for community. We are designed to be family. I cannot wait until He returns, and we can live in a new heaven and a new earth which is an all-inclusive world where our true identity is revealed, and unity is all we will know. Until then, could it be possible that we could see a glimpse of heaven here on earth as His children begin to reflect this eternity God has so graciously prepared for us?

Being color blind is not the answer. The issue is not racism, it is sin and lack of identity. God created diversity, not division. It is through the unity of diversity that God's love and our true identity will be reflected.

Chapter 3: Casting your cares

"I want you to be free from anxieties." 1 Corinthians 7:32 (ESV)

Thanks for watching the kids! I shouldn't be long just going to the grocery store. Oh, the dreaded chore of grocery shopping coupled with the million other things I have running through my mind. I cannot wait to get this task done.

I pulled into the parking lot that day feeling a little edgy. It had been one of those days where my anxiety had been rearing its head. I guess I had too much going on and felt a little overwhelmed. Well, at least I was able to get a fairly close parking spot. As I locked my car door and headed for the store, I jumped as someone pushed their cart into the cart return area. *My nerves are really jumpy* today I thought.

Halfway through my grocery shopping a full-blown panic attack hit me, and I had to leave my full cart of groceries in the aisle and run back to my car. I was so familiar with these incidents now that I did not run in fear to the nearest emergency room, as that would only accelerate my anxiety as they spoke down to me once they realized the real cause for my visit.

Instead, I just sat calmly in the car with the AC blowing on my face trying desperately to calm the million emotions that were raging through my body simultaneously.

Why did this have to be my life? Why is something as simple as grocery shopping unachievable? Why is this disorder so hard to understand?

These, and many more, are questions that I have often about my anxiety and the numerous ways it interrupts my life! It is like a hamster wheel that I am on and can never seem to really make any progress or find an exit to solid ground.

This prison, anxiety, it keeps locked away in a place of fear and uncertainty which cripples your ability to enjoy moments in life. It is like a lingering black cloud on what should be a crystal-clear day at the beach. You cannot enjoy the beauty of the beach or relax in the existing sunshine because you are always keeping your eye on that black cloud waiting for the moment it is going to rain on your parade. It is a confidence-stealer because you cannot trust the moment but are always strategizing how to handle whatever that black cloud is going to spit out. It sucks the joy right out of a situation. You cannot fully enjoy something if your mind is not 100% there, if you are always looking over your shoulder. So many beautiful moments are missed when our daily view is through the lens of anxiety.

The sad thing is it doesn't just affect you and your life, it bleeds out onto those closest to you. My husband had to deal with my anxiety which brought meltdowns over the smallest things. It was like a raging volcano that could erupt at any time, and you never receive warning it just blows, and the hot lava runs all over the people around you. My children were affected by a mom who was, due to her anxiety, overprotective and stifled them from truly enjoying and experiencing life on their terms. I never intended for my children to be raised in a fearful environment and then of course carry that into their adult lives.

Anxiety is a prison that over time you do not even realize you are residing in. I had no idea what a life without anxiety would be like, so my life with anxiety was the only way I knew to exist. The burden of anxiety and the inability to articulate its effects to others is probably one of the most challenging things to navigate through mentally. Those who have never experienced anxiety see it as something you should be able to just not do. If only it were that simple!

I cannot think of a single incident where I would have chosen anxiety to be my companion for the day. I remember the numerous, numerous times I would have anxiety-panic attacks, some of which would lead me to an ER visit, only to have to endure the attitude from the nurses once they realize it was "just anxiety," which only served to fuel my anxiety. Then it was the well-intended lectures received from those closest to me about how I needed to make changes in my life; not take things so seriously, take a deep breath, slow down before I put myself in an early grave. The words were coming from a misguided place of love and concern but again only fueled the fire that was happening in my mind and the feeling of loss control was being confirmed in every word that was thrown my way. It is like trying to get up out of the ball pit, but everyone just keeps throwing balls at you.

I wonder how much of the craziness we experience in life comes from people full of anxiety. What beautiful moments, that are right in front of our face, have we let slip by? How many sleepless nights could have been avoided? How many never-fulfilled scenarios have we played out in our minds and felt in our emotions, wasted time and energy on a "what if" that never played out?

There is a key to unlock the prison door of anxiety and it can be found in our focus.

"Anxiety in a man's heart weighs him down, but a good word makes him glad." Proverbs 12:25.

We do not have to stay bound in the shackles of anxiety any longer! That was never the intent of the Father when he created us. Remember He came so that we can have life and not just ordinary life but life more abundant! The shackles of anxiety were unlocked for me when I began to change my focus.

"Do not be anxious about anything, but in EVERYTHING by prayer and supplication with thanksgiving let your requests be made know to God." Philippians 4:6.

It was when I began to open my Bible on more than Sunday morning and pour the words of His truth into my heart and mind that an intimate relationship began to form between me and my savior, Jesus Christ. It was from within this relationship that I was able to cast my care on Him and truly begin to release my fear and need for control which are the core of anxiety. I switched my focus from my situation and on to the one stable thing I could count on and that was the love of Jesus Christ. His characteristics have been proven trustworthy. It is amazing how much power our thoughts have over us. What you focus on is where you will head. The very atmosphere can change based on the focus of your mind; it is that powerful. As we pour the truth of

God's word into our minds which then penetrates to our hearts it changes the atmosphere. Our circumstances may not change but the way we react to them will, for sure. It was amazing once I discovered this key and was able to unlock this prison door and walk into a day with the ability to enjoy the moments found in it without the black cloud following me. The black cloud may still be there, but my focus is on the things within my control and that black cloud is something Jesus has already considered and provide a solution to.

"So we can confidently say, the Lord is my helper; I will not fear; what can man do to me?" Hebrews 13:6

Anxiety has now become the gauge to let me know my lenses are out of focus. It reminds me that I am missing out on the goodness of God and the beautiful opportunity to trust Him. When that "check engine light" comes on I know that I need to either pick up my Bible and pour in the living water of his word or turn on some praise and worship music to retrain my brain to focus on what is true and trustworthy. God inhabits the praises of His people! Nothing changes the atmosphere in a situation like praise and worship. It also reminds me that communication with the Father is crucial and prayer can be another response to this "check engine light."

There is no magic formula to anxiety being gone forever. There are so many factors that can be contributing to the cause. But what I do know is that if you change your focus and "turn your eyes upon Jesus, look full in his wonderful face and the things of earth will grow strangely dim in the light of His glory and grace!"

Chapter 4: Finding your Place

"But you are a chosen race, a royal priesthood, a holy nation, a people for his own possession, that you may proclaim the excellencies of him who called you out of darkness into his marvelous light." 1 Peter 2:9 (ESV)

The noise of the school lunchroom can be deafening, yet so isolating at the same time. You stand with tray in hand looking for that empty space, that corner of the table where you can sit down without being noticed.

I was that girl, the shy insecure one who no one was inviting to sit at their table. I wanted to be a part of the popular table, but who was I to dare approach the mecca of school cafeterias? Starting school was tough. My inability to find the confidence to speak up and participate labeled me unjustifiably. I found myself in the prison of false beliefs allowing them to become permanent labels that I would incorporate into my very being. The labels ranged from "stuck up" to "goody two-shoes" neither of which were true, but were the made-up assumptions of those who thought it easier to assume than to approach me and attempt to form a bridge, accept a new friend into the group.

Over time, I began to lock myself deeper and deeper into this prison of false beliefs and from its confines lost any ability to regain some self-confidence and find my voice. It seemed like every time I would think I had the courage to walk in confidence the words I would attempt to say would not come out as planned; or worse yet, I would awkwardly approach someone and find myself literally unable to utter a word. This just led to laughter and another shackle keeping me locked away.

School became something I dreaded attending. I felt like I was on the outside looking in, there but unable to fully participate in all that was happening. Still worse was being able to see the side looks and whispering laughter when I would walk by. The best parts of the day for most children, lunch and recess, were the most dreaded for me. In the classroom we all had an assigned seat and a teacher that took the focus off me.

As my school career progressed into my high school years, I attempted to scale the wall that I had built to shield myself. I tried out for the cheerleader squad; I mean if a girl is going to get her gumption go for the gusto! It wasn't a complete fail as I made a squad, just not the football squad, its basketball squad for those who don't quite have what it takes. But hey, I was willing to take it, maybe then I could begin to move from just looking in, to actually participating in this thing called life. A girl can only dream, as I found my awkwardness to follow me to this new place as well.

The unlearned skill of communication and the utter lack of self-confidence left me as an outcast. As usual I was awkward, not fitting in, and then I had a new group of girls to whisper and talk behind my back; sometimes not even behind my back. My closest friend, anxiety stayed dear and true through it all. I earned my lettered sweater because a quitter is one thing I am not. I wish I could say I was proud of that sweater that hung in my closet for years. Heck, it is probably still hanging in the back of my closet today. It does not bring back visions of the glory days for me, it's more a reminder of how much of an outsider I really was.

After that year of trying to be on the inside and failing, I returned to my post in the shadows, observing from a distance and dreaming about how my life could be different if only I had the confidence to believe I had a voice and a purpose and it was ok to exert both. Instead, I chose to quietly finish my high school years as a phantom of the school hallways.

I find it ironic that the greatest feeling of loneliness can be found in the biggest crowds. How can a person get so lost in their surroundings? Feeling as if you have a superpower of invisibility and can navigate through the halls unnoticed, yet able to observe and hear all that is taking place around you. Sometimes even dreaming of what it would be like to be in their place. To live a day in their lives. The thing is no one really knows what another person is going through on the inside.

Masks are something that can masquerade so many demons we want to hide. Lashing out at others is often a mechanism used to disguise insecurities; but as adolescents, we cannot grasp the big picture surrounding us; we know is that life can be awkward and fitting in challenging at times. These brief moments in time seem to be significant in defining our identity. If only we understood the blanket of lies that were being placed on us.

It is funny how the loss of your voice in one season of your life can change the path of your future. How being stripped of your self-confidence can hinder you from walking into your purposefully designed future. Who would have thought that there was so much power in our voice and self-confidence? When did they appoint themselves the authority-makers in our lives?

The key to unlock the prison door of false beliefs is the understanding of who we are in Christ. The truth is our identity does not lie within anything this world has to offer, it lies within our DNA! When we accept Christ, we are adopted into His family and our identity then becomes one of royalty. Think about that for a moment. Let it really sink in deep. You as a child of God are ROYALTY! And who wouldn't want royalty to sit at that table?

There is a certain amount of confidence that just bubbles to the surface at the very sound of the word royalty. All the lies of the enemy are illuminated once you accept your identity in Christ. The fear, shame, and condemnation cannot hold ground when his light of truth penetrates your prison cell. You have a newfound strength even within the confinement of your weaknesses. The truth of God's words of love will become a sword by which you can slay the lies of the enemy.

There will be peace in your steps as you walk into situations with a peace you cannot shake. Faith will replace fear as a shield to deflect the fiery darts of the enemy. The enemy does not want you to understand this royal status that is freely yours for the accepting. He will go to great lengths to keep you locked within the prison he has so carefully crafted over the years. That is why you have to immerse yourself in the words of truth so that it can penetrate into the crevices of your heart and penetrate the depth of your mind; your true identity unlock the prison door and allow you to walk into his glorious day.

At first, the light may be too bright for you to handle; you'll find yourself squinting, thinking that it may be better to return to the dark prison because, although not ideal, it is very comfortable there and your eyes have already adjusted to its condition. Fortified walls have been built around you as a form of protection from the cruel realities of this world, but there is no wall that God won't kick down in His loving pursuit of you! His love is reckless and unconditional. There is no need for anything to be initiated on your end. The King of Kings will stop at nothing to bring his royal son or daughter home!

Every moment locked within this prison cell has been filled with a melody being sung over you, one that your ears were just not able to attune to but nevertheless, it was always being sung. The tears you cried in secret were collected by the hand of God himself! He knows your tears, he understands your struggle; remember, He gave his only son to die on a cross in order to have this kind of intimacy with you. Your tears are not in vain. Imagine the tears you have shed being collected by your loving heavenly Father and being pour together with the tears the Father Himself shed when his son was sacrificed for you! The combination of the two forming a healing stream of water that flows from heaven to earth washing over and running through the broken pieces of your life.

How can you have any false believes about yourself once you are immersed in your true identity as a part of the royal family? God wants to remove the lies and replace them with His words of truth! The mirror He wants you to see yourself through is not dirty and has no cracks, it reflects the way He see you. After all, you were created in their image; the Father, the Spirit, and the Son. You are a unique person. Every detail of who you are from the color or your eyes and hair, to your personality with all its quirks were hand crafted by almighty God himself! The culture you were born into and the era in which you are living are not by chance but by grand design.

What is one of the first things we ask when a baby is born? Do they look like mom or dad? We take great pride in our children and the way they reflect us. Each parent secretly wants the child to look like them as we proudly show off to everyone this amazing newfound love in our lives. God is no less a father! He is so proud of his children! He tells the angels every day "Hey, look that is my son, that is my daughter, see how they are so beautiful and who could deny that they are my child, see how they shine the light of my love!"

That is where our true identity lies, in the truth of our creation and the design of the creator! It is heartbreaking to God when we hide our true identity and try to conform to the worldly description of what normal is. He took great pride and care in creating you uniquely the way you are. He wants you to stand tall and walk proudly as you know will all confidence that you are a child of God and that alone is enough to define your identity. The approval of others is not necessary as you see all others through the loving eyes of your daddy. Your willingness to love unconditionally like your Father makes you lovable. Walking in your true identity shatters the glass walls of comparison as you confidently navigate through life with the full assurance of whose you are. If only we could grasp this incredible truth and teach it to our children what a different outcome it would be for so many. The Father's true purpose for his children would be fulfilled and the abundant life he promises would be a reality instead of a cliché or saying on a coffee cup. Loneliness would not be allowed to exist as we would know that we are never alone; our heavenly father is with us always in all things and through all things!

If we could only catch a glimpse of our true identity, then there would be no shadows in which we could hide because there would be no darkness.

Chapter 5: Sonship

For all who are led by the Spirit of God are sons of God. Romans 8:14 (ESV)

Sitting in a folding chair in this dungy, dusty room stacked with binders of papers so tall that they felt insurmountable, I wondered why I was choosing to go through with this. Everyone seemed to think we were crazy and taking on more than we would ever be able to handle. But these boys needed a home; a real home with a loving family. Their entire life they had been shuffled through the foster care system never being able to find stability and love. Now that they were teenagers the window of possibility was quickly closing. Each one of those binders represented a chapter of their lives in yet another foster home.

As I read each page of those binders, the theme was the same: rejection. The issues they had acquired by their fate in life were the very obstacles that were hindering them from finding a forever family. My heart was pierced by all the failures that had been heaped upon them, a weight that no child should have to bear! They had to feel as if they were drowning in an ocean of despair, as the undertow pulled them back out to sea again and again and again.

I must admit, adopting teenagers was definitely not something that had been on my radar. My husband and I had been foster parents for several years at this point and had fostered more toddler-aged children. When we decided to adopt, our intentions were to adopt a younger child, elementary age at the most.

God had a different plan, and as we dove into the world of adoption, we crossed paths with these two brothers and our hearts were pierced at the sadness of their story. While in the process of discussing potential adoption of these boys, a call came for a potential adoption of a younger, little girl who they believed would be a great match for our family. But, after much prayer, God revealed to us that there was a long line of families willing to take in this little girl, but the line was short--almost nonexistent—for the boys and that is why we should pursue adoption with them.

The initial encounters with the boys went well as they strived to portray a different picture than the reality of their current mental and physical condition. They had many years of practice in the art of salesmanship. My momma heart was so excited to be able to hopefully change the path of these boys' lives! To open our home and allow them to experience the love of family and the love of someone who honestly wants what is best for them. An unconditional love that does not require salesmanship, as if you were a product to be purchased. A love that understands why you are where you are and feels an obligation to help right the wrongs the world has placed on your shoulders.

That was my intention as I excitedly walked into this new motherhood adventure. Little did I know, just because I had something better did not mean they had the ability to accept it. I would soon find myself in unknown territory that would change my excitement into fear as my false beliefs that everyone would jump at the chance for a better life if it was just presented to them was shattered in a million pieces on the floor.

Once we arrived at home with the boys and the "honeymoon" period was over, the true demise of my fairytale ending began. The nightmare began as the acting out and trying to push us away phase was introduced. This phase was destructive and capable of harming our family at times. At one point, a small board with a nail in it was placed on the floor so that when my son jumped down off the top bunk he would have impaled in his foot! It then escalated to scribbling on walls and opening boxes of food and throwing them in the trash! It got so far out of control at one point that we had to have our food in a locked storage bin behind a locked door just to stop the wastefulness and the financial strain that was putting on our family.

The youngest of the brothers was a little more open to the help we wanted to give. The oldest brother however was constantly encouraging him to not listen to us and to stay the course with him. This was a daily battle and one I was not willing to give up on. He had not only the psychological damage but also physical manifestations of the stress and abuse in his life. He was grossly underweight and was on a handful of mood-altering drugs. All of which were just adding to the weight of defeat he was carrying on his shoulders.

We were never really able to penetrate through the walls our eldest son had built around himself for protection. Thankfully, his brother it was a different story. Over time we were able to earn some trust as we navigated through the system of medical and physiological doctors to find a better balance of medications lifting the fog enveloping him. We were able to work him through receiving growth hormones which were right on the brink of being too late to do anything. As we watched him grow and change physically for the better, the mental challenges were more than we could handle.

Meltdowns and an uncontrollable desire to take things that did not belong to him made some of our days beyond challenging. A week did not go by that we were not called to the school for something, but at least he stayed in school; his brother, on the other hand, was expelled from school within a few short months. A scorned, rebellious 16-year-old home all day with nothing to do is a recipe for disaster!

He had a great love for animals and often discussed a desire to become a veterinarian so we talked to our vet to see if he could possibly work at the vet office and shadow the life of a veterinarian, thinking this would encourage him to find a focus on something he loved. We thought he would see it was an attainable dream with a little hard work and determination, and he had the full support of parents who wanted to see him succeed in life. That lasted a few weeks and he was fired from that job. I threw my hands up in the air out of frustration and heartbreak.

Why would he not take the help we were trying to give him? A better way of living was being placed at his fingertips but love unaccepted was not able to move the mountains that were in the way. In fact, the more I attempted to show love and grace the more he lashed out at me verbally, sometimes going as far as threats of physical harm. My mental state was being strained and the health and stability of my family was being altered, so when he came to us with the desire to move in with his uncle until he was eighteen, it looked like a desirable option.

I was torn emotionally as I had such a great desire to show him unconditional love and support. Was this just another test? Should I make him stay and continue to fight for him to accept all the goodness I was trying to offer him? Or could it be that I could not force this love and hope on him but had to let him journey on his own path hoping that the seeds of a different way of life would be deeply planted in his heart and mind and one day he would decide to return and accept the gift?

There were also the feelings of failure on my end. I had so confidently stepped out in faith to take these boys into my heart and home and I felt like a quitter, just another notebook to be added to the story of their failed placements. This was supposed to be different. This was supposed to be the one home that was going to make a positive difference in their lives. But I was worn down, and after much prayer and soul searching, I reluctantly decided to grant him the desire of his heart even though it was breaking mine. I knew he was walking straight into the path of self-destruction. But like it or not, I had to let him make the choice.

It was the beginning of an inevitable destiny for our boys. Although the youngest stayed with us for several more years, he ultimately chose the same path as his brother. This time it was even harder for my momma heart to bear. I had invested more time and energy with him and had seen amazing strides in his physical condition, and his mental state was becoming a little more manageable. Every day was a struggle so I embraced every little victory we could accomplish with great vigor and in those moments, life seemed purpose-filled again, instead of unmanageable and draining.

Just as I thought we were making great strides up his mountain, the rebellion kicked back in and he ran away several times, ultimately requesting to go and live with his brother. We had lost this battle. My dream of making a difference in the life of a child who had been dealt the worst hand was shattered by the reality that they were unable to accept what we had to offer.

There was such a mental struggle over the why! Why would God call me to adopt these boys, just to have it all end in disaster! This was no hallmark movie ending and I felt ripped off! My emotions were all over the place from feeling a failure as a mom to being bitter and angry that God had called me to this place and yet allowed it to fail so miserably! Not only had it failed, but a scar had been left on my biological children who had to endure the emotional turmoil that had become their life.

I had intentions of teaching them unconditional love and understanding; that giving of ourselves in love would produce an outcome that you could be proud of, knowing that having an open mind and heart is not a weakness but a great strength that can change the world. Oh, how devastatingly wrong I had been about everything and how right those voices telling me how stupid this decision was were running the victory lap in my mind with great joy and excitement at the fact they were right.

Deep in my heart I knew there had to be an explanation. God's ways are higher than our ways. I could not see it, but I had to believe that some purpose, that I may not know how this side of heaven had to play out in our lives, but how I longed to see what that was. Catching a glimpse of hope during this war I felt like I had just battled for several years! This soldier was weary and feeling defeated.

In my view there was nothing but defeat and failure. I would look around and see the foster moms and adoptive parents who got it right. Those who appeared to be able to reach their children and make a difference. In the depth of my heart, I wanted to be happy for them and their success, but another part of me felt jealous of the beautiful story of adoption they were able to tell. My story of being an adoptive parent was ugly and unsuccessful. How could I ever encourage someone to be an adoptive/foster parent when I had no basis by which to prove that it was a beneficial thing for these kids.

Obviously, I knew showing unconditional love was the only hope they could ever have; at the same time, though, it was difficult to discuss my failed attempt in the same breath. This became a sore subject in my family. A topic that was hard to discuss because we could not truly understand it ourselves. It had been like walking in this giant bubble of joy, hope, love, and excitement that was quickly and suddenly pricked by a needle and you were sent soaring through the air and landing harshly and unexpectedly on the hard ground of reality.

How embarrassing it was when the topic of our adoption would come up and people would make statements like such as, "Amazing, I could never do that. How incredible! So where are the boys now?" Only to see their expression and feelings towards our endeavor change once we explained the ultimate failure of our journey. Not at all the way I envisioned this calling on my life. It brought so many emotions and so many struggles with all of it, and I was unable to see a purpose or any value that could be expressed from this season of my life.

Have you ever considered the difference between being a child of God and being a son of God? Did you even know there was a difference?

Choice is a gift from God that if not used properly can be the very thing that breaks His heart. Have you made the choice to be a son or are you content with settling into the comfort zone of just being a child?

The prison of complacency keeps us from reaching our God-given potential. It chains us down in a feeling of calm satisfaction with our own abilities or situation that prevents us from trying harder. I would say for a lot of us, it is a lack of believing we deserve anything better.

Within the confinement of these prison walls, we have come to believe that we have reached all the potential possible, and this is the end of the road for us. The mistakes and cards we have been dealt in life, well, they are what they are and there is no way out or around them. Nothing could be further from the truth!

The use of a snake as the representation of the enemy is appropriate. He slithers around whispering lies about our identity and our abilities. Planting seeds of doubt and lies into our minds that prevent us from moving forward. Deceitfully slithering around our circumstances, attempting to keep our focus on the lowly things so that the heavenly things being laid out before us go unseen. It is from the confines of this prison that we begin to accept things as good enough and lose out on the best God had planned for us all along.

The key to unlock the prison of complacency is to choose sonship! To not just settle with being a child of God or a part of the family of God, but to be a son or daughter of the King of Kings and Lord of Lords! It is not enough to just hear the word of God and sing his praises; he desires a much more intimate relationship with his children. A relationship that brings transformations in the sense of being a lost child to a found son or daughter. Walking closely with your father will enable you to feel the very emotions he feels. Remember, Gods word tells us that we will go through the hard times just like we will get to experience the good times.

"But to the degree that you share the sufferings of Christ, keep on rejoicing, so that also at the revelation of His glory you may rejoice with exultation." 1 Peter 4:13

God longs for closeness and intimacy with you. He longs for you to not only be his child, but also accept the position of son or daughter. He knows that within this proximity you can flourish, you can have redemption from your past, you will find protection, you will find agape love. No weapon formed against you will prosper and no scheme of man could ever take you from His hand. His heart literally aches for you, and in the same way breaks for you when you allow yourself to remain in the prison of complacency.

The experience of adopting the boys was a life experience that allowed me to truly understand, on a personal level, the heartbreak and frustration our heavenly Father feels when His adopted children choose to be complacent and stay shackled in the darkness. I began to reflect on this possibility, and it made me take a long, hard look in the mirror. Most of my Christian walk had been as a child or God, not a daughter; the difference is between life and death! Knowing that now, I can see why God was heartbroken at my complacency. While I was operating within it, I could in no way see the beautiful future God had in store for me if only I would choose to accept my place as His daughter. Just like I could see the future for my boys if only they would choose to accept my love and trust my heart was always for their best interest.

Within their walls of complacency, they could not comprehend the things I was trying to get them to believe. The snake was slithering through the situation and for every step that we took forward it seemed ten more would take us backwards. I can just see God looking down on his adopted children desiring with everything within in him for them to accept their place in the family. Not to see themselves as simply adopted but as a chosen part of the family. Understanding the love that it takes to step into someone else's mess and be willing to go to whatever length necessary to clean it up. And by whatever lengths, I mean the sacrifice of one's biological son in order to have the opportunity to have this relationship with you! Only to have us turn our back and continue our own destructive path.

Even through worshipping our adoptive Father, declaring we are his children, and singing his holy praise on Sunday we seem to become fickle and distant in our emotions. God becomes a distant point of pale light in our Monday through Friday "rear view mirror". After everything He has done, all the sacrifice, all the love, all the grace he has poured out, all he has just to be rejected. Unlike me, he never gives up! His unconditional love continues to pursue us even when we run. He is relentless in His pursuit of us, but it still comes down to choice.

Maybe the guilt and failure I was feeling because things did not turn out the way I had envisioned needed to be reevaluated through the lens of choice. I could want the best for the boys with every ounce of my being, but I could not force them to accept that. As much as I wanted to, I could not force them to see the bright future that could be ahead for them. I could relentlessly pursue them, unconditionally love them, never stop speaking truth and light into their lives, but that is where my ability stopped, and their freedom of choice began.

It is the same with us and God; He so desperately desires to redeem and heal us, to give us a freedom from our prisons that only He can provide. The key is in the door, but we have to choose to turn it and walk into the light. God does not want a robot who does what He says, instead, He wants sons and daughters who walks so intimately with Him that they reflect His very character. The beautiful gift of choice leading us into our gardens of life.

I know have a whole new appreciation for the experience that our family went through in our adoption of the brothers. I could have never anticipated its purpose, or even now know that I am completely able to comprehend all God is trying to share with his daughter. I do know one thing for sure, the comparison is eerily similar. I have been given the honor and privilege of walking in the suffering of Christ so that I could be not only a child of the King but his daughter. His spirit connecting with my spirit, in an experience that rocks us both.

The heart God gave me for these boys—remember, I was not looking to adopt teenagers—is the heart he has for us as his children. Even when the world says, "Give up on them they are hopeless,"

God moves toward us with a great passion for his people.

I am pained by the sacrifice of my biological children in the sense that they were exposed to suffering as well, by my choice and not their own. In addition, it appears to be for nothing except the sting of rejection.

God gave the life of His biological son to break down the barrier of sin so that we could become a part of His family, yet how often does he feel the sting of rejection after such an immense sacrifice? The heartbreak I felt at the choice I had to allow them to make even though I knew they could have so much more. God's heart breaks the same when we make destructive choices when he is standing there with arms wide open waiting to welcome his children home.

I am not sure if I will ever see the boys again, or if they are even still alive today, but this experience assures me of one thing, and that is God's love is eternal and He never gives up on His children. A seed was planted in the heart of those boys during the time that we had with them, and I believe in a God who can see to it that they are watered and have potential to grow. Just like God never gives up on us, I will never give up hope that I will see those boys in heaven one day.

I am forever touched by the sharing in the suffering of our heavenly Father, His heart for His children, and His fervent desire for them to accept the position of sonship.

Where do you stand today? Are you a child or a Son? Are you a rebellious teen unable to truly walk in the grace you have been given or are you willing to fully accept the love of a Father that has personally chosen you, in all your imperfection, to carry His name and wear His crown and roar with authority in your life as the son or daughter of the King of the universe with an inheritance that cannot be taken away!

Chapter 6: The Power of Praise

"But he said, 'If they kept quiet, the stones would do it for them, shouting praise.'" Luke 19:40 (MSG)

There is nothing more therapeutic to me than cruising down the road with the sunroof open, the sunshine beaming and a slight breeze blowing in my hair! Whether it's the drive into work, or the unwinding drive home when I need to shake off the dust of the day. Sunshine and music are the perfect combination for a download-recharge moment.

I never really considered the importance of the lyrics I was listening to until a friend challenged me to switch to Christian lyrics for thirty days. I noticed a remarkable change to my attitude. Suddenly, the beginning of my day was brighter and the burdens at the end of my day seemed to wash away, as if in a warm shower. There was power in the words I was implanting into my mind. The message being delivered was more important than the tune it was being sung to. My mind was being expanded and the truth of God's word was making an impact on my spirit and soul. This was an experiment I am glad I chose to participate in, albeit reluctantly at first. This experiment made a critical impact on my life.

I believe this was the battle cry that began my journey to freedom. You see, the mind is the battlefield that the enemy resides on. So, when you are filling your mind with truth and light then battles are being won! It may see like you are just listening to music but the power of the words you are singing and pouring into your battlefield have power beyond anything you could have imagined. It is really a matter of light or darkness. You are either feeding the lies of the enemy or tearing down the lies with the truth, and it's your decision.

It is the subtle things around us that the enemy uses to lure us into the prisons we find ourselves locked in. It is the slow fade of familiarity and complacency that keeps us from moving forward into all God has for us. Music has power, so music combined with the word of God is life changing power. I can attest to that. I am a lover of music. It has always been my go-to when I need a boast in my mood. Heck, I love music playing in the background during my day. Music just does something for the spirit and soul.

When you hear the term Christian music what is your first thought? Did you realize that there is no such thing as "Christian music"? there is only

Christian lyrics that are incorporated into all genres of music. So, to use the excuse that you do not like Christian music is really saying, "I do not like Christian lyrics," which is God's word put to music. Have you ever stopped to think about the lyrics you listen to, and for most of us, memorize in your life and what the message really is? And how that message feeds into your mind, which manifests into your life? Everyone can think of a favorite song, so do that think about your favorite song then really listen to the lyrics and ask yourself, "Is this something I should be feeding the battlefield of my mind? Is this a weapon that can be used to defeat the darkness and bring me closer to the light of truth?"

The enemy is telling you right now that I am overanalyzing music and it is just a fun tune you can listen to and sing along and dance away your cares to. Don't feed into the lie. Those words have power, too, just a different kind of power; one has the power to erect prison walls and the other has the power to demolish them. Which one are you choosing?

Praise is a powerful weapon we so often neglect to use. The book of Psalms is an entire book composed of sacred songs. Isaiah 61:3 tells us God will grant to those who mourn in Zion a beautiful headdress instead of ashes, the oil of gladness instead of mourning, the garment of praise instead of a faint spirit; that they may be called oaks of righteousness. He wants us to have the garments of praise. Just like we get up every morning and put on our "garments" for the day he wants us to put on praise in that manner too.

I don't know about you, but I find it difficult to memorize scripture, but once that scripture was put to a melody of music I enjoy, suddenly I can sing them over and over. They become implanted in my memory and I am able to pull them up when I need them most. God has told us we should hide his word in our heart, and I have found no better way to do this than to listen to Christian lyrics! I cannot tell you how many times I have felt defeated, exhausted, or completely overwhelmed, but then I would turn on some music filled with God truth and a great beat and in no time at all, I would find myself smiling and dancing and praising God.

In the midst of my anxiety and fear I feel as if I am literally being lifted away from my body. I think that is what God is referring to when he says he will give us a garment of praise instead of a faint spirit. The praise replaces the weariness of our flesh with the power of the presence of God in our midst. Psalms 22:3 tells us that God inhabits the praises of his people! When we are singing and listening to praise and worship lyrics we are ushering in the very presence of God. No wonder this thirty-day experiment made such a life altering impact on me.

Now, I have listened to Christian lyrics for so many years, I do not hear the music I used to listen to the same anymore. I still know the lyrics to all my old favorites, proof of my point that these lyrics linger in our mind and make permanent homes, but I do not get the same feeling from them as I do when I praise and worship!

I cannot tell you how many times I have had a Christian song come to mind when I needed to be encouraged or have a boost in my day. God has even placed a song in my mind as a reminder of his truth, oftentimes in preparation for something that was going to rock me in the natural.

God created music and placed within us the love for music. Then He made it our love of the music collide with our need for the word of truth, which transforms into a powerful weapon that can be used to open prison doors and free the captives!

Praise and worship to me is like a moment of heaven invading earth and making sense of all the chaos. It shifts our focus to who and what is really important and changes the atmosphere of the room as we find ourselves in His presence. We connect our mind and spirit to his words of truth and life and a beautiful symphony is orchestrated in the throne room of heaven! Our voices are joining with the angels who are singing Holy, Holy, Holy is the Lord God Almighty!

One of my greatest pet peeves is when the worship time on Sunday morning is treated as a prelude to the sermon. When people drag into church and hang at the coffee counter not seeing any significance to the worship time. The worship is just as significant as the sermon. They are both forms of releasing Gods truth into the hearts and minds of his people. Worship time prepares our hearts and our minds for the sermon. It clears the battlefield of our mind so that the message can be delivered to our hearts. I see worship time as a celebration of all God has done and will do in my life. It is an outward expression of an inward change in my life! I personally don't want to miss a second of the worship time on Sunday morning. Expressing my love and appreciation for the one who gave it all for me, how can you not want to participate in something like that!

Remember the high and happy feeling you get when at your favorite concert singing at the top of your lungs, whether you can carry a tune or not, and the words you are singing are making you feel carefree, releasing emotions pinned up on the inside? That is the same energy we are releasing in true Sunday morning worship at church. The only difference is that the words we are singing out carry a divine power to change us on the inside and not just make us carefree but truly free!

Songs can also pierce us in a personal way. There are so many songs that we can relate back to a certain time or event in our life, even years later when we hear that song our mind and emotions go back to that place and relive that moment in time whether good or bad. Christian lyrics can evoke the same emotions, the difference is the words of these songs are alive and breathing and sharper than any double-edged sword! They pierce us in a way that brings breakthrough and change to our lives. They also can remind us of where we have been and where God has taken us to. Some of them are like anthems we can sing loud and proud as we have been busted out of prisons!

There is nothing old school about Christian lyrics; they are powerful and gut wrenching and the perfect way to implant scripture in our hearts for future reference. Most of Paul's ministry was from prison, where he chose to do what? Sing praise and worship songs! If worship ushers in the spirit of God, then it evicts the enemy because he cannot be in His presence.

Why would we not arm ourselves with the weapon of praise that God has so graciously afforded us? This is a concealed weapon that you don't need a permit to carry. It is always at your disposal.

Music + scripture = eternal power.

Don't neglect the weapons that you have been given for the spiritual battle. The weapon of praise will break down walls and shatter strongholds! I encourage you to take the thirty-day challenge I took. What have you got to lose? Your music will still be there when it's over. I can guarantee that if you truly stick to the challenge and surround yourself with praise and worship music for thirty solid days, there is going to be a noticeable impact on your life because you will find yourself in the presence of your Savior. The words that will begin to penetrate your mind will find their way to your heart and the chains will begin to rattle as you are set free from the prisons of lies and sing yourself right into the arms of God.

Chapter 7: Dating without Identity

"But the Lord said to Samuel, 'Do not look on his appearance or on the height of his stature, because I have rejected him. For the Lord sees not as man sees; man looks on the outward appearance, but the Lord looks on the heart.'" 1 Samuel 16:7 (ESV)

I hated the feeling I experienced more times than I care to recount. Driving to the night club where we used to frequent, I desperately hoped what I was imagining in my mind was not what I was going to witness when I arrived. Pulling into the parking lot I began to feel the anger and frustration build. Why? Why is it that I have such horrible taste when it comes to choosing men? What is it about me that says, "Cheat on her, she doesn't desire any more than that"?

This time, could I be wrong? Just once could it be that the man I was with valued me enough to stay true? As I entered the club and smelled the familiar smell of alcohol and the blaring music that was luring me to the dance floor, I began to make my trip around the room to see if there was any sign of him with this mysterious woman. Halfway around the room and no sign of them yet, could this have all just be my paranoid self?

If only that had been the case. As I rounded the next corner, I caught a glimpse of him cozied up to her without an ounce of guilt at the double life he was leading. I froze in the moment not knowing if I should march right up there and get in his face and let her know the truth. Did she know the truth or was he deceiving her, too? About that time his eye caught mine and the sheer panic on his face let me know she was in the dark. He frantically started making his way over to me to ensure that he cut me off at the pass before his little escapade was blown out of the water.

I quickly turned and ran out of the building tears running down my face out of pure anger this time. I had reached the point of being pushed over the edge. A girl can only take so much heartache before she cracks and crack I did. Shy and timid, I'd been walked on for the last time. I decided to retaliate in the only way I felt safe doing so.

The one thing that was precious to this want-to-be a cowboy was his truck, so that is exactly where I headed to release my anger! It felt amazingly freeing to kick the headlights out! The sound of the shattering glass shook me out of the anger trance I found myself in and I looked around to see if anyone had witnessed this act of vengeance. The coast was clear, so I decided it best to leave the premises as quickly as possible while I was still ahead. Driving home I imagined what was going to happen when he walked out and found the broken glass on the ground. I am sure he had some woman scorned story to tell his latest catch and if she was anything like me, she would buy it hook, line, and sinker.

Have you ever found yourself in a destructive cycle when it comes to relationships? Do you feel like you are a magnet for the wrong guy? Looking in the mirror, do you question, "Will I ever find true love or am I even worthy of it?" These are definitely thoughts that have run laps through my mind! Until I met Jesus and my perspective was changed.

I can relate to the story of woman at the well found in John 4:4-26. She was coming to the well in the heat of the day just to avoid the other woman who typically went in the cool of the morning. Why? Because she was the talk of the town. Her record with men was not a good one. She had been married five times and she was currently the Samaritan living with another guy to whom she was not married. The cycle she found herself in was like a hamster wheel you could not find the exit to. One failed relationship after another had left her defeated and low on self-esteem. It was bad enough that she was a woman in that day and time, and a Samaritan woman at that, so she was being ostracized within an ostracized community. How is that for a double whammy?

I can feel her pain and rejection as she arrives at the well to draw her water for another day. Thinking, as she wipes the sweat off her forehead, "How did this become my life?" She lowers the bucket into the well wondering if she will ever truly be able to quench this thirst for love and acceptance in her life and then Jesus arrives on the scene.

A Jew. A male. Two very big reasons why she expected nothing from his presence. In fact, I believe she was feeling frantic on the inside. Perhaps she was thinking, "I need to get my water and leave as quickly as I can."

Then she hears him speak to her. He said, "Give me a drink."

She had no way of knowing the power that was about to be unleashed through these four little words! She was finally visible and not in the way that she had been avoiding but in a genuine way with an unconditional love that she had only imagined in her wildest dreams. The day had come when someone would accept her in all her mess and offer her a truth that would free her from the endless cycles of shame and guilt. This day was no ordinary day! She was in the presence of her creator and He was able to see the family resemblance.

He knew she was created in His image, therefore He was able to see beyond the current mess that her sin nature had created, instead he looked into the beautiful reflection of the Father she truly was. He knew that the cleansing water he was going to administer to her that day was going to penetrate deep into the soul and bring lasting change and renewal to her life. He loved her so immensely that He planned this divine encounter on this specific day knowing her hiding place. This woman at the well is not given a name in scripture, and that is what makes it even more relatable. It leaves the blank name tag for you to write your name on today.

Jesus didn't just meet that one woman at the well. No, He has an abundance of living water that he wants to pour into every woman that struggles, that hides, that feels less than, who cannot find her voice. He knows your "well," that place you go to find fulfillment or maybe just to drown out the thoughts that are on repeat in your mind. God never intended us to be imprisoned by our mistakes or shackled by a lack of self-worth. Until we truly understand the relentless love God has for each and every one of us, we cannot fully understand our true identity. Operating outside of our identity in Christ leads to imprisonment in a repetitive cycle of bad choices.

How did this seemingly insignificant story make the cut to be a testimony in the Bible? Because God knew the prison of insignificance could not be left unopened. He thought you were worth it. He was willing to break all the rules to reach your heart and loosen your chains, allowing you to walk in your true identity because he knew it was going to impact every aspect of your life. He didn't die so you could walk in insignificance, He died so you could have life and not just ordinary life, but an abundant life found in our true identity.

Dating is one of those areas that can be extremely dangerous if navigated through the prison walls of insignificance. Darkness attract darkness, but the darkness cannot exist in the light. We are children of light; therefore, darkness will no longer be drawn into our path once we own our identity. See the significance? See the life altering path that this living water can provide?

I have had my encounter with Jesus at the well! He has met me in all my mess, failed marriages, and living with men I was not married to. He has offered me the living water which has quenched the thirst I could not fill on my own. Just like the woman at the well, who after her encounter with Jesus left her water bucket and ran into town unashamed, full of confidence to proclaim the change her encounter with Jesus made in her life! No longer hiding in the shadows but now running front and center to share the good news of hope and freedom that could only be found in one man at that was Jesus Christ!

I am writing this truth in full transparency so that all that will listen can hear and witness the freedom found in Christ! I no longer want to hide in the shadows and allow shame and guilt to shackle me down. I have been forgiven and I have been cleansed! I no longer run after or hold onto relationships to quench my thirst but know my value which then attracts men who value me. Do you need to make a trip to the well for a long drink of living water? Jesus is patiently waiting for your arrival.

Chapter 8: Freedom from the Shackles of Shame

"Each one will be like a shelter from the wind and a refuge from the storm, like streams of water in the desert and the shadow of a great rock in a thirsty land." Isaiah 32:2 (NIV)

Laying in my room exhausted from the deceptive game I had been playing, thoughts of total despair overwhelmed me. Warm tears began to run down my cheeks as I struggled with the reality of the person I had become. I was living out everything I knew to be wrong and the shame and guilt of it all was crushing down on me like an avalanche. I had been granted a second chance in my marriage, yet I found myself doing everything in my power to destroy it. I didn't even know consciously why.

What had brought me to this place? How could I sit in church with my family on Sunday and Monday through Saturday live a double life of sinful pleasures? Why was my moral compass being thrown so far off course by my sinful nature?

If this continued, I was not only going to shatter what little is left of my marriage, I was also going to hurt another family that does not deserve this pain. I had to turn the corner. Things had to change. The phone call had to happen so that I could jump off this train before it goes over the cliff. My only worry is how I would stay off this course and be able to stand firm in changing my ways and embracing the gift of a husband I had right in front of me.

This was the moment I found my personal rock bottom! I found myself out of my bed and lying face down on the floor crying out to a God I was not sure could hear me anymore or would even want to. I was ashamed and shattered and this was my Hail Mary; my last grasp at hope for the love and family I dreamed of in the depths of my soul, but I did not feel it was something I deserved to have especially in the midst of my unfaithfulness!

Have you ever felt your failures have permanently defined you? That no amount of good could possibly erase the bad choices that you have made? What if that wasn't true? In fact, what if your shame could be changed into glory? Your mess become a message of hope and light?

What if?

I stood up and made a pact with God. I was going to surrender to Him and not look back.

However, this unfaithfulness was going to be our little secret because what good could ever come from my husband knowing the truth?

God allowed this pact to stand for several more years but not forever because an omitting of the truth still constitutes a lie and every lie will be illuminated in time. God had a plan and a purpose for the release of the truth but in the meantime, He had a work He wanted to do in me and my husband individually, so that the release of the truth would bring healing and strength to our bond. One of the beautiful things about God is His love which covers a multitude of sins. There is no distance you can go that is too far for God to reach you. He wants to be your shelter and refuge, your water in the desert, and the rock on which you can firmly stand.

I had no idea how to begin this relationship with God, but I knew that it was the only way I was going to be able to stay on the right path. Numerous attempts had been made in the past to do so within my own strength and you see how well that had worked.

This time was going to be different. Insanity is doing the same thing expecting a different result. I no longer wanted to act insane, so I began my new way of doing things by starting out with a quiet time each morning. I set my alarm to get up a half hour earlier and spend that time in God's word while my house was silent, and my mind could be focused. It was a struggle at first because I had no idea where to begin reading or even how to understand what I was reading. It took discipline and self-control to continue getting up and delving into God's word. I found some devotionals that helped structure and guide me through this process of opening my Bible outside the church building.

They say you create a habit after twenty-one consecutive days of doing something and that is exactly what happened with my devotional time with God. The habit began to turn into a form of communication between God and myself. It was like a therapy season where the therapist was making a home visit. We would sit together every morning with our cup of coffee, and every day we grew closer and closer. I began to feel His presence and the words of the Bible started to become very real and relatable. It was a dialogue between two great friends. He knew everything about me, and I was getting to know Him more and more each day. The words of the devotions and the scriptures that were leading me started to have such personal implications to my life. They were like a healing salve that were ministering to my wounds. There were tears of joy and tears of pain, as sometimes the bandages had to be ripped off so that the healing could reach the deepest wounds.

The more I read the words of truth, the less I wanted to stray away from them. A foundation was built under my feet and it kept me on the right path. As our friendship grew and the depths of His love were revealed, I began to want to emulate that same love to those I came in contact with, including my husband. Things were beginning to make a turn for the better, at least from my perspective. I could feel myself changing in the way I felt and the way I acted. There was a lot of work to be done but I was no longer self-destructing. I felt as if I was being reconstructed from the deepest parts of my being.

There was a message God wanted me to not only hear and read but also to apply to my life. Through this relationship, God wanted me to see myself the way He sees me. In order to do that, he needed to convict me of the things that needed to change in my life. This was so much different than the condemnation I had felt in the past, when my faults were pointed out to me.

His conviction was loving and encouraging, like when we want our children to make the right choices but we have to word it in such a way that they do not feel like we are dictating to them what to do but lovingly leading them in the right direction. That is the way God convicts us. I had to face some ugly truths so that I could begin to see the beauty God wanted me to see in myself. The shame and regret had been the defining factors in my life and God was about to turn that upside down.

These powerful words were spoken over me, "Your shame does not define you, I do." This concept of God defining me instead of my shame and regrets had never entered my mind before. It was like a river of water flowing through a desert land. My perception had always been that my shame and regret not only defined me but confined me from being able to reach God. He wasn't going to have anything to do with a wretch like me. I was operating under religion which says you must do or be instead of relationship which says come as you are. God is not looking for perfection just a heart seeking Him. That heart can be broken, rotten, cracked, scarred and barely beating. With one touch from the Savior and it can be whole again!

I had to hit rock bottom before I could ground my feet on the rock that does not move! His love cannot be undone by anything we have done. His grace is sufficient for all our mistakes. Do not stay in the prison of shame and regret. Your Abba, daddy, Heavenly Father is waiting for you to surrender to Him.

Remember, he is not seeking perfection but progression. He wants to make you more and more like him every day. To take your from glory to glory to glory. To bring beauty from ashes! It is a metamorphosis. Moving from the natural to the spiritual realm, yet never leaving the ground. It is a healing and restoring like nothing you could imagine in your wildest dreams. That is why God wants a relationship with us! It is a connection with the one person, Jesus Christ, who can change everything!

The enemy deceives you every day, telling you that you've gone too far, that there's no way to turn around. He keeps you locked in the shackles of shame and regret unable to move forward in a new direction. God, on the other hand, is whispering His truth over your life hoping that you will hear the calm, quiet voice that is calling you to join him for a cup of coffee. He wants to be your friend, your confidante. You will experience the Bible in a whole new way, the words will have life and they will guide you in this journey called life. Life will not be perfect because perfection is not attainable this side of heaven, but it will bring peace and hope and clarity to the bumps in the road of life. You will begin to understand that all things can be used for our good and His glory.

I could not fathom how my marriage could be restored and my family kept whole but God could. What feels insurmountable to you right now? Could this be your personal rock bottom? Because it is at rock bottom that you can meet the eternal rock and stand tall and firm on His foundation. He is the anchor that holds us steady through our storms. Where we find on the other side restoration and healing that allows His glory to shine in the midst of our sins.

Chapter 9: Eternal Perspective

"But godliness with contentment is great gain. For we brought nothing into the world, and we can take nothing out of it." 1 Timothy 6:6-7 (ESV)

I will never forget that day, driving over the mountain to what I thought was going to be just another day at work. I received a phone call, and ironically, I found myself sitting outside the cancer center where I worked hearing the voice on the other end of the phone saying the word cancer. I felt that heavy weight that makes it impossible to take your next breath.

I was surrounded by cancer and cancer victims all day long but this time it was personal, this time it was my dad. My entire world turned upside down. I felt as if I was having an out of body experience, things were still moving forward as normal, but somehow, I could not process things normally.

Every cancer patient that walked through the front door that day took on a whole new emotional meaning to me. Things viewed through the eyes of personal experience definitely changes the clarity of your view. That day was the beginning of a six-month journey that lead to the passing of my dad, and a change of perspective for me taught in one of the lowest valleys I have ever found myself walking through.

A little girl's love for her daddy is something that is hard to describe with words and losing them is completely indescribable! Inevitably we know our parents are going to pass in our lifetime, but it is never something you can truly prepare for. Knowing my dad was dying of cancer did not make the day of his death any more bearable, but it did show me in a whole new light the characteristics of my dad that I loved and miss so much.

Dad was a family man to the core he loved any excuse for a family gathering. He also had a mischievous sense of humor, and even as an adult, he relished instigating trouble. He also had a very serious side and was a good listener. He had a servant's heart and was always showing us by example how to lend a helping hand whenever we could. A man who brought an essence of grace to any room he entered. Now, he was gone and a piece of my heart along with him. The only way I was able to sustain during this season was because of my relationship with my Heavenly Father. I was too weak to bear such a heavy sorrow, but there was a lesson to be learned in this season: an adjustment of perspective and focus.

Have you ever been on a walk and taken the time to really look at the beauty around you? Take some time to smell the roses or notice a beautiful sunrise or sunset? Maybe you have driven the same roads day after day but one day something catches your eye and the beauty of it draws you in, then you realize that you have passed by it every day for weeks and never noticed it. That is the best way I can describe what I am going to share with you about a lesson in eternal perspective.

There is a prison that I believe we can all find ourselves in and that is the prison of worldly vision. It is a dangerous prison because it clouds our ability to see life as the temporary journey, and it makes us think that this is it. If we do not conform and perform to the world standards, we are told, then we are destined for failure and unhappiness. The key to unlock this prison door is found in a new perspective one in which we measure things from our eternal destination instead of our temporal location. This was never made more applicable to me than in the experience of my dad's journey from this temporary world to his eternal home in heaven.

Several days before the call came telling me my dad had cancer, I had been humming a song I had heard in church that Sunday called The Rock Won't Move while on lunch break at work. It wasn't something I typically did in front of other people and one of my co-workers asked what I was humming. I hadn't even realized I was humming, and I answered surprising myself. I wondered to myself why I was humming this particular song.

It immediately arose to mind again when I received the news. The Rock Won't Move and His love is strong. The Rock Won't Move and His love can't be undone! Jesus had been preparing my heart for the news he knew was going to rock me. He wanted to remind me in advance, plant deep in my heart and mind that He was the rock, my foundation, no matter what storm had just begun to brew. To instill it even more a patient came in that same week with a CD she had made called The Rock Won't Move. I was undone by the storm and the Savior who loved me so much that He was sending reminders and confirmation to keep my focus on the eternal truth not the temporal condition my family found themselves in.

My parents were living in Florida at the time, while my brother and I both lived in different states. Wondering how I was going to be able to take time off and go to Florida to be with my dad weighed on my mind daily. His diagnosis was right before the holidays, so we of course made trips to Florida for

Thanksgiving and Christmas. Things were not getting better and time with him was not guaranteed, so my brother and I both came to Florida to stay with our parents.

It was during this time that God began to shift my perspective of the situation. It was hard to know that my dad was going to deteriorate daily and not know when he would take his last breath. I could not have mentally made it through this time had it not been for my early morning hours with Jesus. It was during this time that He was able to comfort me and begin to turn my eyes toward the eternal truth. It is not very often that you get the opportunity to have the time to spend with your love one before they pass. Although it can be one of the hardest things to process and navigate through, I began to see the blessing in the four of us being together as a family again. It was like returning to where it all started and the look on my dad's face when he would see us all in the kitchen getting ready for dinner was priceless.

I dare to imagine what he must have been thinking and reflecting on during those days. He did not want us dwelling on his impending death but wanted to make the best of the time he had left while he still had the wits to do so. Being a photographer by trade, he wanted to capture some fun memorial moments one last time. One of the best memories was when my brother and I "kidnapped" him to take him down to the beach for the day. When we got settled in our chairs in the sand, Dad pulled out this handkerchief and says to tie it around his mouth and use the chair bag to tie his hands so we could send a picture to my mom letting her know he had been kidnapped.

I still have the picture from that day and remember fondly the childlike behavior of my dad, and how he made us all smile amid such sadness. He was laughing so hard. Those are the moments I have chosen to keep tucked deep in my heart. Or the picture of my dad in his wheelchair with me holding it with one hand and an umbrella in the other like Mary Poppins while my hubby was pulling my foot to "keep us from blowing away".

I was somehow able to sustain and maintain while not working for a month. Nothing more than a blessing from God in providing a way for me to have this precious time with my dad. There is no doubt this was one of the hardest things to experience with a love one, but it was through the pain that I was able to see the gain.

Death is not some sort of punishment or end all. Oh, no! Death has been defeated by our resurrected savior! Death is just the door that leads us home! I prayed earnestly and tearfully for the healing of my dad! I believed and knew that God was able to turn this all around. But his form of healing was not the form I was anticipating but it was healing all the same. My dad passed through the thresh hold of heaven and all things were new! Although I do not have my dad here with me on earth any longer, I have the peace in knowing where my daddy is and that it was not goodbye but see you soon.

God's goodness did not stop there. He did not forget his daughter and the loss she was feeling. He gave me signs of comfort to help me keep my eternal perspective. I had a dream in which I saw my dad in heaven, and he was around a campfire with a bunch of guys who were laughing and telling tales. He glanced over at me with that distinct smile of his and my heart knew he was in a better place where there was no more pain.

One more time God graced me with the comfort of knowing my dad was indeed healed and happy. One day, while doing my daily walk to the hospital to check the mail, the most beautiful butterfly landed on my hand and would not fly away. It literally stayed with me to the front door of my office where I had to coax it onto a bush before I went in. My dad had made me a screen door with butterflies carved into it before he passed. My heart was so full of love and hope that day.

85

This whole experience has changed the way I see this journey called life. This is our temporary home; we are just passing through on our way to our eternal home. Death is not the end it is the beginning of a new life a perfect life! Every time I find myself missing my dad I just look up in the sky and say miss you dad and cannot wait to see you again. It is like he is in a foreign country and I am just waiting on my passport so I can go see him.

What is your current perspective? Are you caught up in the things of the world that bring temporary satisfaction? Do you know Jesus? Do you know your eternal destination? Death was defeated on resurrection day! It no longer has any power over us! Accept the gift of eternal life!

"For I consider that the sufferings of this present time are not worth comparing with the glory that is to be revealed to us." Romans 8:18

It is in our deepest pain we can experience the most intimate relationship with Jesus. It is like our pain is a door that leads us one step closer to the throne. When Jesus says our pain does not compare to the glory to come, he means our pain has purpose, if we will allow it to take us to a place where we can feel the very presence of God in the land of the living. He is not minimizing the very real, very raw pain we are experiencing. He himself wept when his friend Lazarus died, even knowing he was going to raise him from the dead in just moments. He still took the time to release the emotion in the midst of the glory that was about to shine in it. Part of His heartbreak was also in the fact that His friends had to experience the pain of death before there could be the power of resurrection. So, He wept with them.

Our God is the same yesterday, today, and tomorrow so there is no doubt in my mind that Jesus weeps with us in our pain also. He is with us arms wrapped around us, shedding tears alongside us in our grief knowing that joy comes in the morning, when all the pain is erased, and our glorified bodies are given in replace of our weakened human condition. Our loved ones will experience their Lazarus moment!

God knows our pain and grief in the loss of someone we love. He has felt the unimaginable pain of not only losing His one and only Son but being the one to sacrifice Him so that we would no longer have to fear death.

I can relate to the pain and anguish that Martha felt when Jesus arrived "too late" to save Lazarus. My heart felt the same tug of war as hers when she said, "Lord, if you had been here, my brother would not have died." I too was confused as I knew God had the power to heal my dad if only, he would have come to his rescue. Yet from an eternal perspective this picture can be seen more clearly.

God said, "I am the resurrection and the life, whoever believes in me, though he dies, yet shall he live, and everyone who lives and believes in me shall never die." God wants us to understand that a believer's life is an eternal life! Death is just the exit from our physical bodies to our spiritual bodies. Death was defeated and has no power over us! It is not something to be feared but something we see as the finish line of a well-run race.

Philippians 1:21 tells us, *"For to me to live is Christ, and to die is gain."* Our hearts should yearn to be with Jesus because we know that it will be so much greater than our finest moments on earth. Paul tells us in this chapter that he is hard-pressed between the two. His desire is to depart and be with Christ, for that is far better, but to remain in the flesh is more necessary on your account. This is the type of eternal perspective that we should be living in our lives. Our hearts should be in a tug of war between bringing souls to Christ and going to see Christ ourselves. Nothing on this earth is worth staying for when the glory of eternal life is at hand. Our perception of death reflects our perception of life. We really are in a win-win situation, we either get to stay here with more time to spread the gospel of Christ or we get to go to our eternal home and be with Christ! Both admirable in their own right.

"When a woman is giving birth, she has sorrow because her hour has come, but when she has delivered the baby, she no longer remembers the anguish, for joy that a human being has been born into the world. So also, you have sorrow now, but I will see you again, and your hearts will rejoice, and no one will take your joy from you." John 16:21-22

This scripture reminds me that there is pain prior to gain. Jesus had to experience the pain of the cross in order to have victory over death and make the gift of eternal life possible. Women have pain in bringing new life into this world. There is also pain in the opening of the door that leads us to our eternal home. But in all incidences the pain is worth the gain.

Chapter 10: Waiting on God

"I believe that I shall look upon the goodness of the Lord in the land of the living! Wait for the Lord; be strong, and let your heart take courage; wait for the Lord!" Psalm 27:13-14 (ESV)

Squinting at my email with a fresh cup of coffee in my hand, hoping that this would be the day I would get the answer I was longing for. My early morning routine for months now had been to wake up, grab coffee, and check my emails (also known as find a job).

The jobs were there but the number of applicants was great. You had to catch it when it first posts and then hope you could make it through the screening process to the hiring person. Two things seem to be obstacles I could not overcome, my age and not being bilingual.

Then the morning jewel appeared in my email: a job opening that was scripted for me! It was in the field I had been working in previously and my experience and expertise would override the desired bilingual requirement. Not only was it perfect but the early bird gets the worm as it had just posted a few hours ago! This was looking very promising. The excitement from the possibility of a job interview was more energizing than the coffee I was drinking.

Within a few hours I was contacted to set up an interview! This came at the beginning of the COVID-19 quarantine so it would be a phone interview. The morning of the interview I arose with excitement as I really had a good feeling about it. It was so perfect and surely this was God sent. Right before time for the call the lawn maintenance crew arrived to mow the grass! Are you kidding me? So, I went to the quietest place in my little duplex which was the bathroom and waited for the phone to ring.

I laughed at the thought of what it looked like for me to be in the bathroom with my phone and note pad ready for an interview. Three minutes before the call was supposed to be made, I received a text message apologizing but informing me that the interview was cancelled the position had been put on hold until the COVID-19 quarantine was lifted. I was very disappointed but still held hope that when it opened back up then we would pick up where we left off, but hopefully not in the bathroom the next time!

Fast forward 3 months and the job market was starting to move again. I was eagerly anticipating that job to reappear but, in the meantime, I was of course applying for every opportunity I could find. Jobs started opening again and opportunities were coming in but not as good as the one I had before the quarantine. I needed to get back to work so my desires would have to take a back seat as I needed some income again.

I remember during my prayer time with God this thought flooding into my mind. *That phone call that got cancelled at the last minute that was me stopping you from taking something good when I have something better planned for you.*

Could I believe this thought running through my mind? And would that better look like? I began to ponder that and list my desires for a job. One of my greatest desires was to work close to home, as over the years I have had to travel long distances to work every day. With the traffic in our current location, close to home was high on the priority list. Of course, I was seeing very little opportunity in my desired field that was close to home.

I began to hold onto the words that had been placed in my mind and often pondered the possibility that something good—maybe even great—could be coming my way. The calls started coming in for interviews and I prayed before each one not wanting to desperately grasp at the first opportunity, but to ask the Lord if this was the one or should I wait.

I had several interviews within one week and had narrowed down one that would be a good job but did not meet my desire to work closer to home. I had my first initial phone interview, which went very well and was set up for my second interview in a few days.

In the meantime, I got a phone call for a job I had applied for that I had forgotten about in all the applications I had submitted. It met all my desires for a job including being only 13 minutes from my house! I went for this interview the day before my second interview with the other company was scheduled and was hired the same day. God had been faithful to the words he had spoken to me earlier. He did have something better than I could have foreseen, becoming a reality. In my mind, I had imagined the ideal job scenario, and He had made it come to life. I am so glad he made me wait for the better instead of settling for the good. That is what happens when we wait on the Lord! We get to experience the things we cannot see a way of accomplishing began to unfold right in front of our eyes.

In the world today, instant gratification is a predominate desire in our lives. Have you ever stopped to think about the things you may be missing out on as you fly through life full speed ahead?

Do you wonder if there are blessings left behind on the side of the road because you were driving too fast to see them there?

If we could just slow down, take a deep breath and take in all that is around us. Really look at the blessings currently in your life and dream about the possibilities that have not even begun to play out yet. God's timing is not our timing. He works off a different clock than we do. His timing is perfect. Our timing is often impatient and impulsive.

The prison of instant gratification keeps us from God's best in our lives. In this prison, you strive not thrive. You try to fill the voids in your heart with the things of this world, which will never be able to bring long-lasting fulfillment. The key to unlock the prison door of instant gratification is to learn the reward of waiting on God. We often think about the goodness of God and all the blessings he has promised in His word as something we will experience after we die and get to heaven. Then and only then will we see the goodness of God manifest in our lives.

But that is not what God's word says. His word tells us that we can see the goodness of the Lord in the land of the living. We do not have to wait till we die to experience his goodness, but we do have to wait. The word wait just seems to bring on so much frustration not to mention actually doing the waiting.

We are so wired to want to have it right now(!) that we lose out on the benefits found in the waiting.

Waiting is not some kind of punishment God conjured up to watch us suffer. Waiting is so much more complex than that. It can be a season of rest. It can be a season of growing and developing. Sometimes the miracle God wants to perform in your life just takes time. Time to prepare for what the Lord has waiting in your future. Time to heal some old wounds so you can walk into your purpose whole and prepared. Time to slow down and walk with Jesus, he so enjoys your company. Time to surrender.

I can personally guarantee that you will never regret the wait. It will not always be easy to wait, especially when you believe you have all the answers and know what's best from your own limited point of view. But as you wait and receive you will begin to trust in the waiting process. I have so much life-changing testimony of waiting on God.

Seven years ago, we took a huge leap of faith and uprooted our life in Florida and moved six-hundred miles away from our young adult children to North Carolina. It was there that God did a great work in our marriage and our family as a whole. Our first grandchild was born three years ago, and when he was born, I did not really want to wait on God to allow me to move back to Florida to be closer to him. This Memaw yearned to be closer to him. But I knew God wanted me to wait so I choose to wait.

I write this book today from my duplex in Florida. Two and a half years after my grandson was born, and I found out I had two granddaughters on the way, God flung open the doors for us to return to Florida and keep our home in North Carolina. I had decided to reignite my crazy faith in believing the seemingly impossible and God in his perfect timing made it possible.

None of what I am experiencing now would have been had I taken things in my own hands and moved too soon. The perfect job opportunity for my husband opened up in God's timing not ours. Difficulty in finding a rental with our dog was remedied in God's perfect timing. Where God guides, he provides, and He has been faithful to that promise to us. Even during a pandemic, we have flourished! If we wait on God, we will get the privilege of experiencing his goodness in the land of the living.

Right here, right now we can catch little glimpses of heaven in the blessings God provides in His perfect timing. In the waiting, God has been strengthening my faith muscles and teaching me to slow down and rest in His presence. After experiencing His goodness, you begin a new habit of asking Him before making a move because you do not want to settle for good, you want to wait for greatness.

Just because something is good does not mean it is from God. Wait on Him. Ask him if this is His best for your life. Waiting is a gift not a curse. Don't let the enemy deceive you into believing otherwise. Worship God in the waiting. There is no better way to grow your faith than to worship God in believing in what you cannot see. That is the very definition of faith. Full Assurance in True Hope. Know that the waiting has purpose.

God has your best interest at heart. He wants you to experience His goodness in your everyday ordinary life! His love is pouring over you in the waiting. Think of it like you did as a kid waiting for Christmas day in anticipation of all the gifts that would be under the tree that morning. God wants your life to be like Christmas morning, full of surprises and gifts you never dreamed you would find under your tree. Cross the days off the calendar as you wait on God with great anticipation knowing that so often the longer the wait, the greater the reward. Waiting should bring excitement and anticipation knowing that if he says no, wait. Then something even better is up ahead and who wouldn't be excited about that?

Never forget that God is with you in the waiting, he does not leave you to wait alone. He encourages you and loves on you in the waiting. There is strength to be found in the waiting, strength that will carry you from glory to glory. Declare that you will wait on the Lord and see what happens. He is faithful and His word is true.

"But they who wait for the Lord shall renew their strength; they shall mount up with wings like eagles; they shall run and not be weary; they shall walk and not faint." Isaiah 40:31.

"And they overcame him by the blood of the Lamb and by the word of their testimony." Revelation 12:11

My prayer is that the words of my testimonies have collided with the blood of the lamb and broke open prison doors in your life. God has declared the power of testimony and the release of them!

I pray that you will come to experience the love God wants to lavish on your life and believe that He is pursuing you right where you are!

May the words you have read bring a new perspective of Jesus and His healing power. He wants you to have life and life more abundantly!

Take the keys! Open the prison doors and find true, long lasting freedom on the outside!

Bibliography

Scripture verses marked ESV are taken from the English Standard Version.

Scripture verses marked NIV are taken from the New International Version.

Scripture verses marked MSG are taken from The Message.

Portion of the song Turn Your Eyes Upon Jesus were quoted.

Portion of the song The Rock Won't Move were quoted.

Tracy McFadden is the founder of Illuminate the Dark ministry which was inspired by her newfound freedom in Christ. She is a writer and encourager who loves to share her testimony to enlighten the path to freedom for others. Through transparency and vulnerability, she desires to rattle chains and breakdown the prison walls that so many people find themselves confined in.

Made in USA - North Chelmsford, MA
1179521_9798689348278
10.13.2020 0828